HOW YOUR BODY WORKS

READY FOR ACTION

BONES AND MUSCLES

THOMAS CANAVAN

PowerKiDS
press

Published in 2016 by
The Rosen Publishing Group, Inc.
29 East 21st Street, New York, NY 10010

Cataloging-in-Publication Data
Canavan, Thomas.
Ready for action: bones and muscles / by Thomas Canavan.
p. cm. — (How your body works)
Includes index.
ISBN 978-1-4994-1230-7 (pbk.)
ISBN 978-1-4994-1253-6 (6 pack)
ISBN 978-1-4994-1244-4 (library binding)
1. Musculoskeletal system — Juvenile literature.
I. Canavan, Thomas, 1956-. II. Title.
QP301.C218 2016
612.7—d23

Copyright © 2016 Arcturus Holding Limited

Produced by Arcturus Publishing Limited,

Author: Thomas Canavan
Editors: Joe Harris, Joe Fullman, Nicola Barber and Sam Williams
Designer: Elaine Wilkinson
Original design concept and cover design: Notion Design

Picture Credits: All images courtesy of Shutterstock, apart from: Science
Photo Library: p10 middle (Michael Abbey). Lee Montgomery and Anne
Sharp: back cover, p30, p31.

Manufactured in the United States of America
CPSIA Compliance Information: Batch #WS15PK:
For Further Information contact Rosen Publishing, New York, New York at 1-800-237-9932

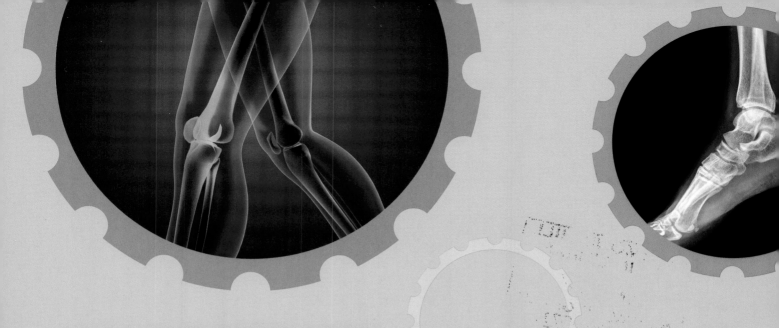

CONTENTS

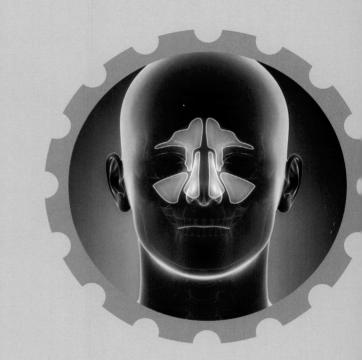

READY FOR ACTION

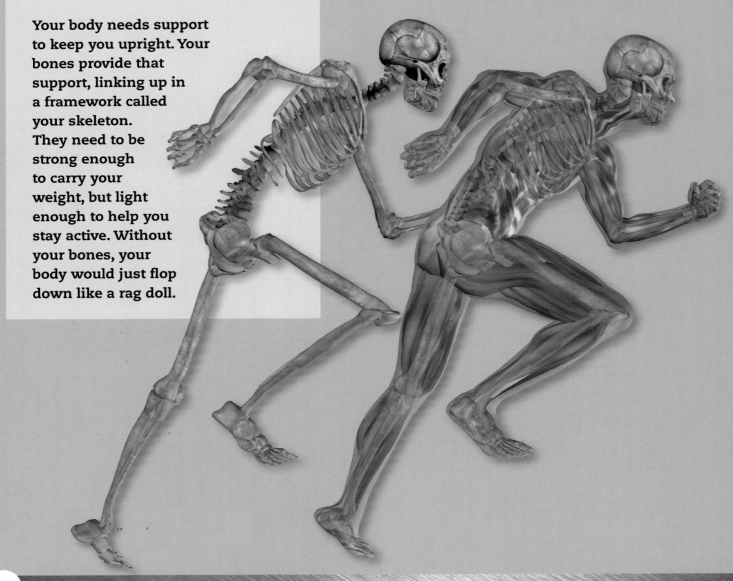

Your body needs support to keep you upright. Your bones provide that support, linking up in a framework called your skeleton. They need to be strong enough to carry your weight, but light enough to help you stay active. Without your bones, your body would just flop down like a rag doll.

It's one thing being able to stand upright, but you also need a system to hold your bones together and to guide them. That's the job of your muscles. You call on them every time you need to move – whether it's picking up a piece of paper or running in a race. Behind the scenes are other muscles that work day and night – automatically – to keep your body functioning.

Your skin does more than just cover your body like a huge sheet of wrapping paper. It keeps you warm or cools you down, and it acts like a cushion to protect what's inside. It's waterproof and it protects you from the sun's most harmful rays.

THE SKELETON CREW

Skull

Ribs

Backbone

Humerus

Your skeleton is your body's framework – a scaffolding of bones that gives you support, just as strong metal girders support a skyscraper. Your bones give your body its shape and structure.

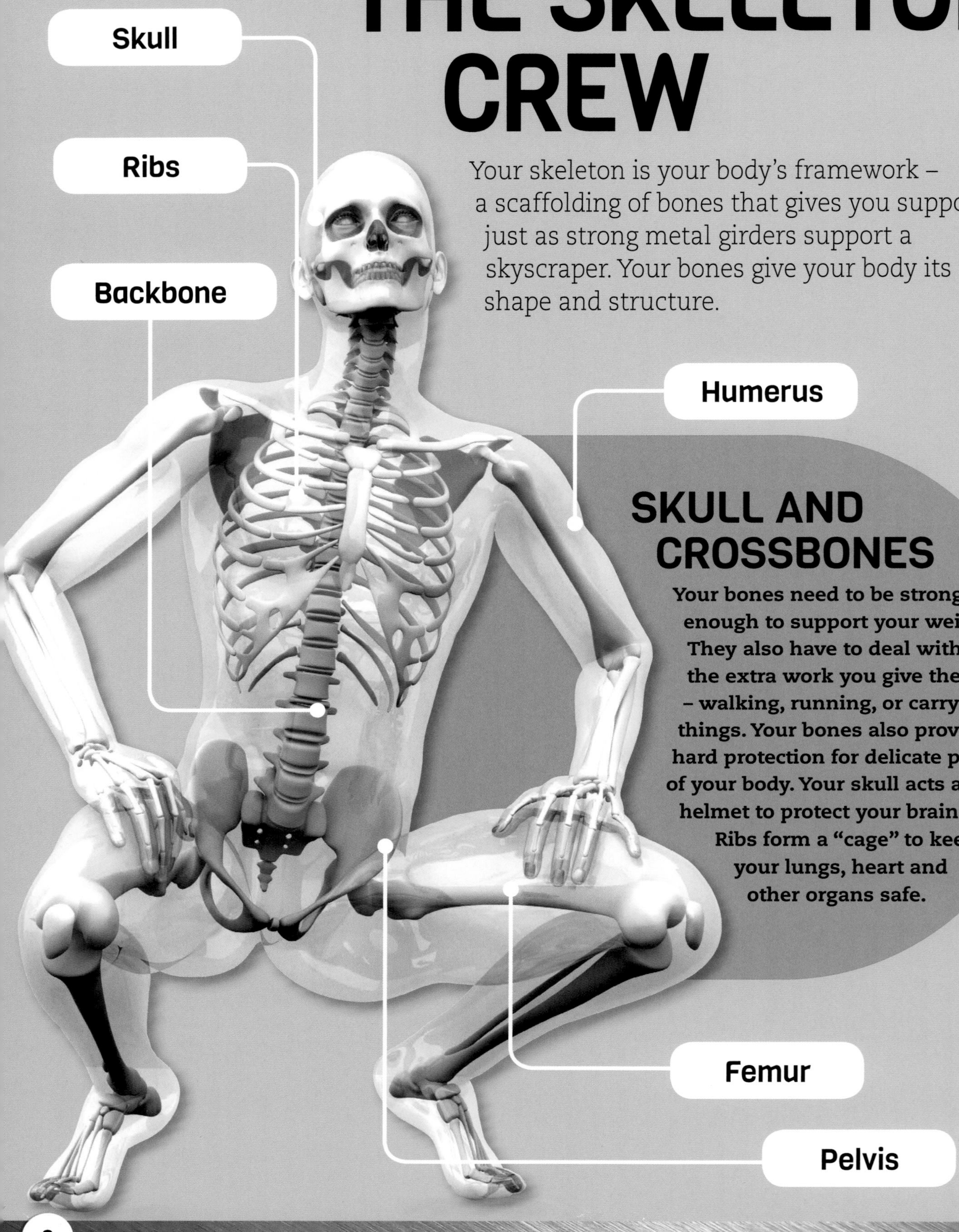

SKULL AND CROSSBONES

Your bones need to be strong enough to support your weight. They also have to deal with the extra work you give them – walking, running, or carrying things. Your bones also provide hard protection for delicate parts of your body. Your skull acts as a helmet to protect your brain. Ribs form a "cage" to keep your lungs, heart and other organs safe.

Femur

Pelvis

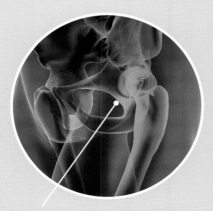

Ball-and-socket joint

JOINT ACTION

Joints are the junctions where your bones meet. Some are fixed, which means that the bones on either side stay in place. Others, like the elbow and knee, are called hinge joints. They move like the hinge of a door. Ball-and-socket joints at your shoulder and hip allow one of the bones to move much more freely – almost in any direction.

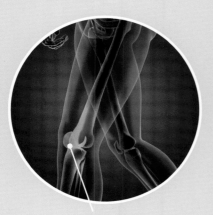

Hinge joint

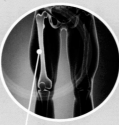

Femur

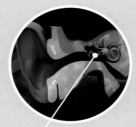

Stapes

BIG AND SMALL

The femur, the long bone in your upper leg, is the largest bone in your body. It needs to be that big because it absorbs most of the force when you walk or run, or even stand. The smallest bone in your body is the stapes. It's only as big as a grain of rice and is found inside your ear. The stapes is one of a series of bones that picks up vibrations in the air and helps us to hear sounds.

Your ribs move each time you breathe. That's 5 million times each year!

FUNNY BONE

If you bang your elbow, it can give a sharp, stinging pain called "hitting your funny bone." But what's hurting is a nerve called the ulnar nerve. Most nerves are protected beneath bones and muscles, but this nerve is close under your skin by your elbow.

TYPES OF BONE

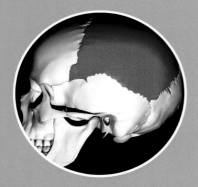

Flat bone (parietal bone in skull)

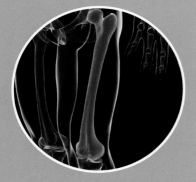

Long bone (femur)

Sesamoid bone (patella)

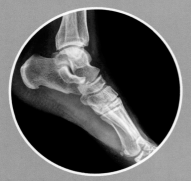

Short bone (tarsal bones in foot)

THE HARD STUFF

Your bones need to be very strong to stand up to the stresses they will meet throughout your lifetime. They also have to be light enough so you can move freely around. But your bones are not the hardest parts of your body – those are actually your teeth.

SHAPE UP!

When you were born, you started out with about 300 bones in your body. Some of those fuse, or join, together to become larger bones. An adult ends up with 206 bones. These bones have a spongy inside, called marrow, and a hard outside made of a chemical called calcium carbonate. What a bone does plays a part in how it's shaped. For example, flat bones are excellent protectors. Long bones support your moving limbs. Sesamoid bones help the junctions, or joints, between other bones. Short bones give you support without actually moving.

BLOOD FACTORY

Bones do more than just support and protect you. There is spongy marrow inside your bones which acts like a factory. Marrow produces blood cells that your body uses for energy, to fight disease and to help you heal.

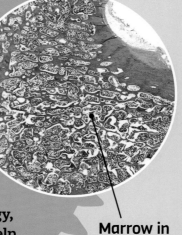

Marrow in a hip bone

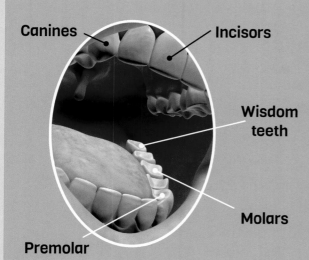

Canines
Incisors
Wisdom teeth
Molars
Premolar

THE DAILY GRIND

If you want to see the hardest bits of your body, then just look in the mirror and smile! Throughout your lifetime, your teeth will cut and grind their way through thousands of meals. Like bones, their shape depends on their job. Incisors and canine teeth cut and tear food into smaller bits. Premolars and molars grind that food. Wisdom teeth are an extra set of molars that come through the gum when you're around 20 years old.

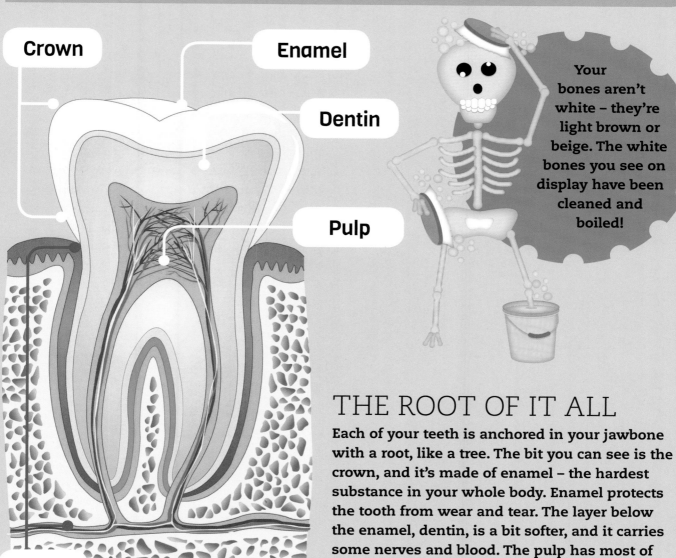

Crown

Enamel

Dentin

Pulp

Root

Your bones aren't white – they're light brown or beige. The white bones you see on display have been cleaned and boiled!

THE ROOT OF IT ALL

Each of your teeth is anchored in your jawbone with a root, like a tree. The bit you can see is the crown, and it's made of enamel – the hardest substance in your whole body. Enamel protects the tooth from wear and tear. The layer below the enamel, dentin, is a bit softer, and it carries some nerves and blood. The pulp has most of the nerves and it sends signals to your brain, such as a painful toothache – ouch!

MEAT ON THE BONES

Muscles are the parts of your body that let you move around when you stand up, lift a box, or kick a ball. You can consciously tell some muscles what to do, but that is only part of the picture. Muscles also help to digest your food, make your heart beat, and make you breathe. You don't need to consciously tell those muscles what to do.

MOVE IT!

Your skeleton is the framework that keeps your body supported, and your muscles allow that framework to move. The type of muscles that move bones about are called voluntary muscles. First, you think about what movements you want to make. Then, your brain works out which muscles are needed and sends messages to those muscles. The muscles move, and so do you!

Muscles make up **40%** of your body weight.

40%

WIDE-EYED

Muscles also help you see. Smooth muscles in your eyes work constantly to focus on whatever we want to look at. They close up the pupil in bright light and open it up in dim light. They react faster than any other muscle in the body.

There are more than

600 muscles

in your body! These range from the large gluteus maximus muscle in your rear end, to the tiny stapedius muscle in your ear.

stapedius
actual size

ACTIVITY

Dim the lights. After a few minutes, look at your eyes in a mirror. You'll see that the pupils in the middle of your eyes are bigger. Brighten the lights and look again. They should be smaller. Your eye muscles have contracted, or shrunk, to keep out the bright light.

You have **THREE** types of muscles:

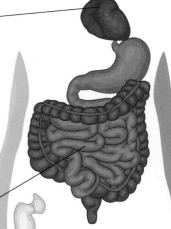

1

CARDIAC
These make up your heart and keep it pumping.

2

SMOOTH
These make up your guts and intestines.

3

SKELETAL
These are attached to your bones and work with them to move your body.

MUSCLE POWER

When you think of your muscles, you probably think about the ones you use to hold a pen, do a push-up, or ride a bike. Those are your voluntary muscles, the ones that you can direct. They're also called skeletal muscles because they are connected to your bones.

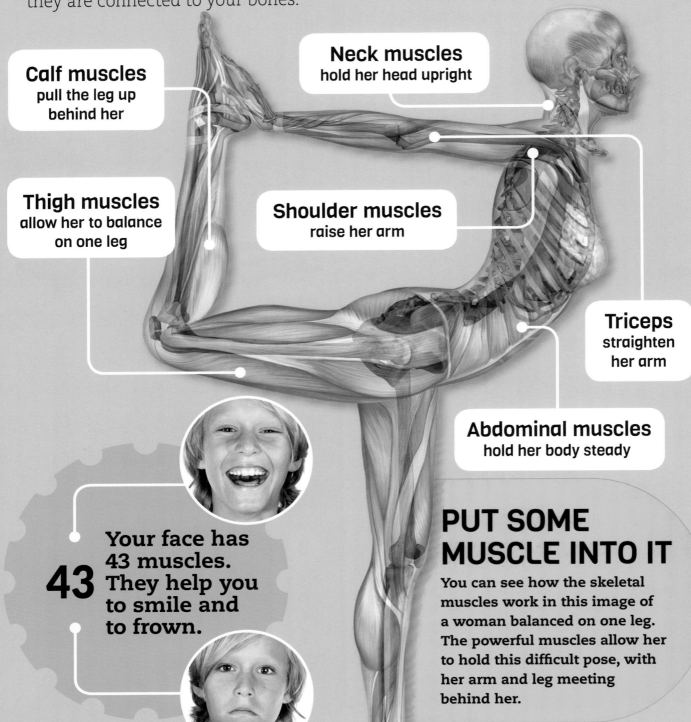

Calf muscles
pull the leg up behind her

Neck muscles
hold her head upright

Thigh muscles
allow her to balance on one leg

Shoulder muscles
raise her arm

Triceps
straighten her arm

Abdominal muscles
hold her body steady

43 Your face has 43 muscles. They help you to smile and to frown.

PUT SOME MUSCLE INTO IT

You can see how the skeletal muscles work in this image of a woman balanced on one leg. The powerful muscles allow her to hold this difficult pose, with her arm and leg meeting behind her.

WORKING IN PAIRS

Muscles work in pairs that pull in opposite directions. They never push. Muscles contain a protein called actin. When another protein, myosin, sends a message to the actin, the muscle tightens up, or contracts. So when you show off and flex your arm muscles, it's the biceps muscle on the top side of your arm that pulls your lower arm up. When you straighten your arm, the triceps muscle on the other side pulls it back down again.

If all the muscles in your body pulled in one direction, you'd be able to lift

25 tons!

That's the weight of a whale!

ACTIVITY

Hold your right arm straight out in front of you. Count how many times you can open and close your fist in thirty seconds. Now, rest for fifteen seconds and try it again. The second number should be smaller because your muscles will be tired out!

BREATHING HARD

Muscles use oxygen from your blood supply to get energy. Normal blood flow allows you to continue with steady exercise, such as walking. But if you're more active, your muscles need more energy, and use up more oxygen. That's one of the reasons why you breathe harder when you exercise – your body is trying to get more oxygen.

WORKING NONSTOP

Your voluntary muscles sometimes get to take a break. For example, your tennis match might have ended or you've just finished the last lap in the pool. But there are other muscles in your body that are constantly working. They are your involuntary muscles, which keep your body ticking over. Cardiac muscles have kept your heart beating since the day you were born, and smooth muscles work with lots of organs inside your abdomen.

You don't control your involuntary muscles. The ciliary muscle in your eyes works automatically to help you to focus on objects both near and far!

W
E H
A V E
R E M O
V E D A L
L T H E R U
D E W O R D S

Smooth muscles contract and relax constantly in the iris of your eye

ON DUTY 24/7

Involuntary muscles work all of the time, even when you're asleep. They work inside your body and help your body's systems to remain on duty for 24 hours of the day!

Cardiac muscles keep your heart beating

Smooth muscles keep the airways to your lungs open

ABDOMINAL WORKOUT

The muscles in your abdomen are pretty amazing!
Not only do they protect your internal organs, but they
also help you to breathe and support your spine. The
ones that help you swallow and digest food are called
smooth muscles. They don't have the striped look of
the much stronger voluntary or cardiac muscles.
There's an advantage to this smoothness.
These muscles can squeeze and stretch
in all different directions.

Lining of
intestine

Smooth muscles

Smooth muscles in
your bladder relax as
it fills with urine

Smooth muscles squeeze
and relax to help food
through your intestines

Smooth muscles react to
the pressure in the walls
of blood vessels to control
the flow of blood

TYING IT ALL TOGETHER

It's one thing having a skeleton to keep you upright. And it's another to have a set of muscles to move those bones around. But you need a few more elements to tie those systems together and make them work smoothly. That's the job of your cartilage, ligaments, and tendons.

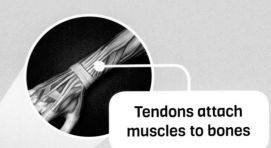

Tendons attach muscles to bones

ALL JOINED UP

Muscles wouldn't be able to move your body around if they weren't joined to your bones. Tendons, which are like cords made of tough tissue, link your muscles to your bones. Cartilage is a bendy tissue. You can easily find some cartilage in your body – try touching the bit in your nose between your nostrils. Cartilage acts as a shock absorber where bones meet at the joints. Joints also have stretchy straps (like tight rubber bands) called ligaments, that connect the bones.

Cartilage acts as a shock absorber between joints

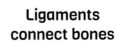

Ligaments connect bones

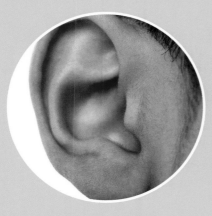

BEND AND STRETCH

Cartilage moves easily. That's why you can bend your ears (which are made mostly of cartilage) without hurting them. Cartilage is a good cushion to nestle between bones because it's soft. Your bones started as cartilage. As you grew, new cartilage formed at the ends of your bones. That cartilage itself turned to bone, getting longer and longer, until you finally stop growing.

A human tendon is strong enough to hold a small car without tearing!

ACTIVITY

Fold your hands so your fingers cross over each other. Then, straighten the ring finger (next to the little finger) of each hand so their tips touch. Ask a friend to put a coin between these fingertips. Now, try to pull those fingers apart. You can't – because your tendons are pulling in the opposite direction.

CLOSE CONNECTIONS

Ligaments are short bands of tough, fibrous tissue. They connect bones to other bones to form a joint. They also prevent some joints from moving too freely. If you've ever twisted your ankle, you'll know what it's like to have a joint that moves too much.

SKIN DEEP

You probably think that your skin is just . . . well, skin. The important stuff is all inside, and the skin is the packaging, like the plastic wrapper on a new birthday card. However, your "birthday suit" is one of the busiest parts of your body – a waterproof, living coat that protects you.

THE BODY'S BIGGEST ORGAN

Your skin does a lot more than just keep your body covered up! It protects you from infection, keeps your body at an even temperature, and lets you have a sense of touch. And when you think of how much of you it has to cover, no wonder it's your biggest organ.

Hair shaft

Epidermis

Dermis

LAYERS

Skin has three layers, but you can only see the outer one, the epidermis. It's constantly at work, producing new cells to replace those that die away. Beneath the epidermis is the dermis, which has blood vessels such as capillaries. Sweat glands and hair follicles (where hairs are anchored) are also found there. Below the dermis is a layer of subcutaneous (which simply means "below the skin") fat, which cushions and keeps your body warm.

Subcutaneous fat

Hair follicle

COOLING DOWN

Have you ever seen steam rise or evaporate from a surface? The water has turned from a liquid to a gas. It's the same when you exercise. Your body produces a liquid called sweat through tiny pores (openings) on your skin. As it becomes a gas, the sweat evaporates, taking some of the heat with it as it leaves your body – so you start cooling down.

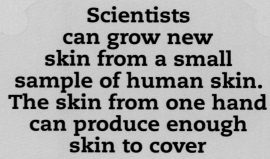

FRECKLED SKIN

Your skin produces a substance called melanin to protect you from the sun's harmful rays. That's why your skin darkens if it's exposed to the sun. Sometimes, that extra melanin clumps up instead of being spread around, which is why some people get freckles. Although your skin does protect you up to a point, it's important to wear plenty of sunscreen as further protection from the sun.

WARMING UP

Your skin can "shut the door" on sweat pores as easily as it opens them. Your body produces extra heat when you begin to shiver in the cold. Shutting your sweat pores is a way of keeping that heat inside you!

Scientists can grow new skin from a small sample of human skin. The skin from one hand can produce enough skin to cover

36 Olympic swimming pools!

TOUGH AS NAILS

Did you know that not every part of your body is alive? Your hair and nails – at least, the parts that you can see – are made from dead cells. They are formed from a tough protein called keratin, which is also found in the hooves and horns of animals. They do not contain any nerve endings, which is why you can cut them.

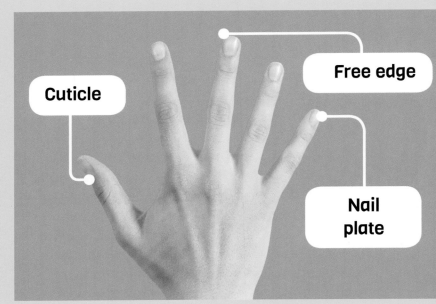

Cuticle

Free edge

Nail plate

NAILED IT!

Your nails do two different jobs. They protect the sensitive ends of your fingers and toes from painful bumps and bruises. They also help your fingers to move things around, by giving a stiff backing to the soft tissue of the fingertip. The top part of your nail plate (the main body of your nail) is made of layers of dead tissue. Beneath it is the matrix, from which the nail plate grows.

Fingernails grow four times faster than toenails!

STOP CHEWING YOUR CLAWS!

Why do you have nails and not claws at the ends of your fingers? You can thank your tree-climbing ancestors. Their claws shrank into nails to give their fingertips more of a feel for the safety of thin branches.

KEEPING A COOL HEAD

The type of hair you have is all down to your genes. In the same way that people have light or dark skin depending on where their ancestors lived, hair types are also linked to sunlight and heat. Curly hair protects the head from the sun's harmful rays better than straight hair. It also allows air to move through it easily, helping you to keep cool.

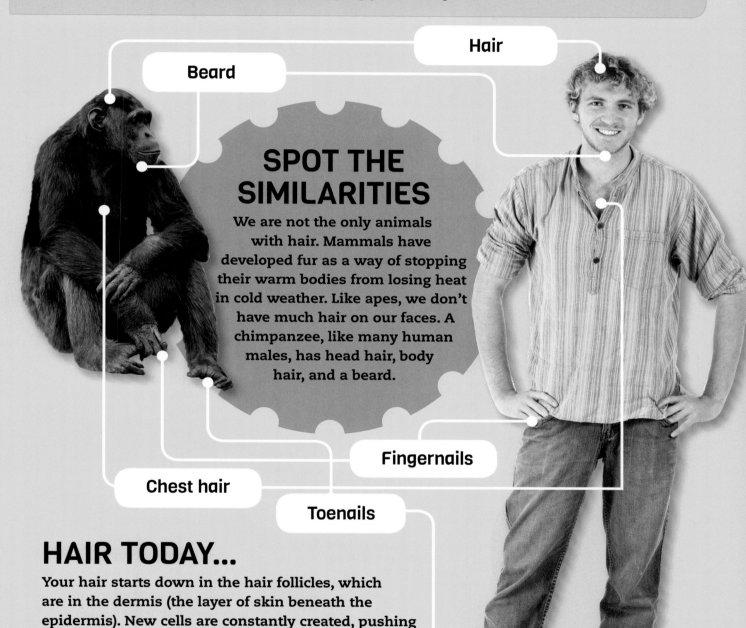

Beard

Hair

SPOT THE SIMILARITIES

We are not the only animals with hair. Mammals have developed fur as a way of stopping their warm bodies from losing heat in cold weather. Like apes, we don't have much hair on our faces. A chimpanzee, like many human males, has head hair, body hair, and a beard.

Fingernails

Chest hair

Toenails

HAIR TODAY...

Your hair starts down in the hair follicles, which are in the dermis (the layer of skin beneath the epidermis). New cells are constantly created, pushing older ones out and up. A layer of keratin (the same substance as your nails) forms around these dead cells, which gets pushed further out. Some men's hair follicles shrink over time, meaning no hair gets pushed out, and they begin to go bald.

SPARE PARTS?

If you think of your body as a machine, then there must be some spare parts. These are the bits that don't get used so often, even if they once served a real purpose. That's because, over millions of years, human beings have changed or evolved.

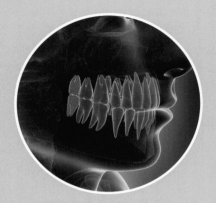

WISDOM TEETH

Humans once needed these extra teeth to chew roots and raw meat.

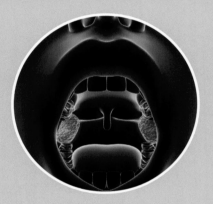

TONSILS

These help to fight infections, but you can manage without them.

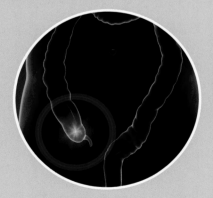

APPENDIX

Scientists used to think this organ was useless. Now we know it can help kill germs in your gut.

NO JOB TO DO

Why do men have nipples? After all, they can't breastfeed babies. The reason is that we all develop in the same way in the first few weeks in the womb, and we are all following the instructions for being female. It's only after a few weeks that boys start to follow different, "male" instructions. By that time, everyone has nipples, and boys and men keep them, even though they have no job to do.

BLASTS FROM THE PAST

Other parts of your body, such as your tailbone (coccyx), appendix, and wisdom teeth, are reminders of how we may have looked and lived millions of years ago. Back then we were hunting mammoths, chewing raw plants and climbing trees. You can think of them as fascinating links with the past.

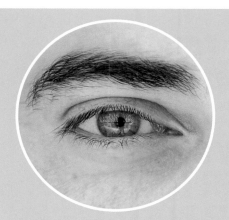

EYEBROW SLEUTH

Here's a chance to play medical detective. Why do you have eyebrows? And why might human beings have needed them in the past? One theory is that they stop sweat flowing into your eyes from your forehead. Another is that they are important for communicating emotions to people around you. What do you think?

ONE BIG HEADACHE?

Some bits of your body remain a mystery, and no one is really sure what they were ever meant to do – even in the distant past. Your sinuses are a good example. They're the hollow bits in your head behind your nose and cheeks. They can give you a terrible headache if they get infected, but no one knows for sure why you have them. The latest theory is that sinuses stop your head from being too heavy – because air weighs less than bone!

The coccyx is the lowest part of your backbone. It's the remains of a tailbone from our distant ancestors!

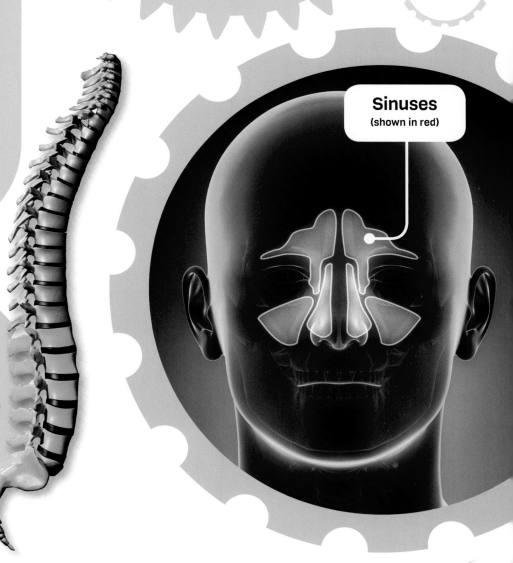

Sinuses
(shown in red)

DID YOU KNOW?

A QUARTER OF YOUR BONES ARE IN YOUR FEET

Why so many? Think about it. Your skeleton has to support your weight, and all that weight is transferred down to your feet. But in order to move freely, you need lots of small bones rather than big, chunky ones. So each of your feet has 26 bones – to help you move and to support the rest of your body.

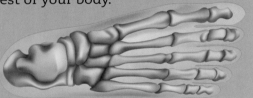

YOU HAVE THE SAME NUMBER OF HAIRS ON YOUR BODY AS A CHIMPANZEE

The difference is that your body hair is much finer and harder to see. And although human body hair doesn't provide a thick coat, it still has some jobs to do – especially to warn you if insects or other tiny creatures are crawling over you.

YOUR THUMBS AND FINGERS DON'T HAVE ANY MUSCLES

The bones in your fingers and thumbs are attached by tendons to muscles in your hands and forearms. It is these muscles that move your fingers. You can see the tendons at work if you hold your arm out, palm facing up, and wriggle your fingers. The muscles that power your fingers are incredibly strong – just watching a climber on a steep rock shows you just how strong they need to be.

THE HYOID BONE IN YOUR NECK IS UNIQUE

That's because this horseshoe-shaped bone is the only bone in your body that's not attached to another bone. The curved part follows the shape of the neck as it meets the bottom of your jaw. Although it has no joints with other bones, the hyoid bone helps support the trachea (windpipe) as well as muscles in the jaw.

YOUR EYE MUSCLES CONTRACT AND RELAX ABOUT 100,000 TIMES A DAY

Just think about how often your eyes have to focus and re-focus. Every time the light changes, or you move, or something moves in front of you, the muscles in your eyes respond. If your leg muscles had to work that hard, it would be like walking two marathons every day!

IT TAKES A FINGERNAIL UP TO SIX MONTHS TO GROW FROM BASE TO TIP

Most fingernails grow at about 0.12 inches (3 mm) a month, although the bigger nails (like the index finger) grow a little faster than the smaller fingernails. Toenails are even slower. It takes 12 to 18 months for a new toenail to grow fully.

DO HAIR AND NAILS CONTINUE TO GROW AFTER YOU DIE?

Old folk tales – and today's zombie movies – would have you believe that hair and nails carry on growing, but the truth is a little different. Hair and nails stop growing, just like everything else, when someone dies. But as the tissue on the head and fingertips loses moisture, it shrinks a little, so more of the hair and nails become exposed – possibly making it look as if they are still "growing."

WHAT CAUSES A SPASM IN YOUR SIDE WHEN YOU EXERCISE?

The honest answer is no one knows for sure. It probably involves the diaphragm, the large muscle that controls breathing. One theory is that the muscles doing the hard work (exercising) divert blood that would have gone to the diaphragm. The diaphragm then starts to cramp (move in a sudden and painful way). Another explanation is that undigested food below the diaphragm gets sloshed around by the exercise, causing ligaments leading to the diaphragm to get sore.

WHICH MUSCLE IS THE QUICKEST TO GO INTO ACTION?

That prize goes to the orbicularis oculi, the muscle that encircles the eye and causes the eyelid to close. You've probably noticed its quick reaction time – about 0.01 second – if an insect flies close to your eye or a branch swings back as you walk past. What's more remarkable is that the signal to react begins at the eye, when it sees the insect or branch, then zooms to the brain and back again – all in a tiny fraction of a second.

WHY DO YOU HAVE TOES?

Although humans can no longer grasp objects easily with their toes, as monkeys and other apes can, your toes serve a very important purpose. First, they help keep you balanced. Your big toe supports about a quarter of your weight, and your other four toes support another quarter – the heel does the rest. Second, they help push you off on each step. Ever watched a gymnast doing a flip on the beam? That would be impossible without toes.

SYSTEMS OF THE BODY

Skeletal system

The skeletal system supports and protects your body.

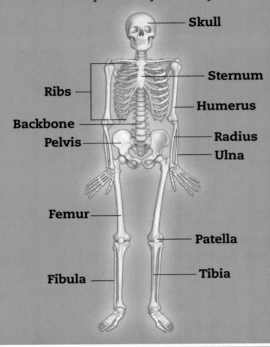

- Skull
- Sternum
- Ribs
- Humerus
- Backbone
- Radius
- Pelvis
- Ulna
- Femur
- Patella
- Fibula
- Tibia

Muscular system

The muscular system moves your body.

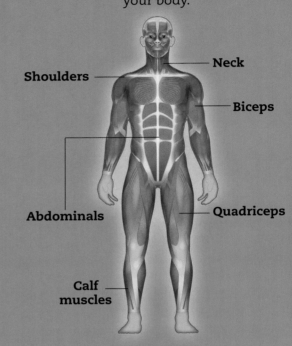

- Neck
- Shoulders
- Biceps
- Abdominals
- Quadriceps
- Calf muscles

Circulatory system

The circulatory system moves blood around your body.

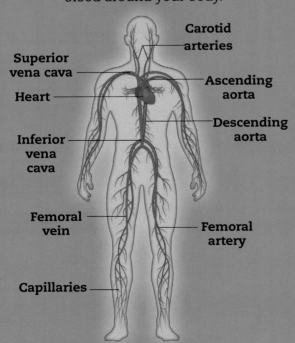

- Carotid arteries
- Superior vena cava
- Ascending aorta
- Heart
- Descending aorta
- Inferior vena cava
- Femoral vein
- Femoral artery
- Capillaries

Respiratory system

The respiratory system controls your breathing.

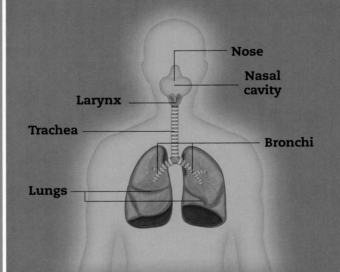

- Nose
- Nasal cavity
- Larynx
- Trachea
- Bronchi
- Lungs

This is your quick reference guide to the main systems of the body: skeletal, muscular, respiratory, circulatory, digestive, nervous, endocrine, and lymphatic.

Digestive system

The digestive system takes food in and out of your body.

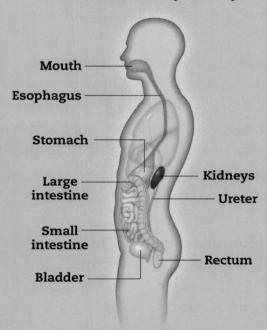

- Mouth
- Esophagus
- Stomach
- Large intestine
- Small intestine
- Bladder
- Kidneys
- Ureter
- Rectum

Nervous system

The nervous system carries messages around your body and controls everything you do.

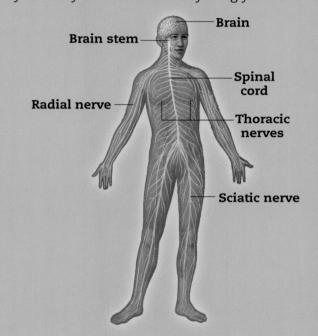

- Brain stem
- Radial nerve
- Brain
- Spinal cord
- Thoracic nerves
- Sciatic nerve

Endocrine system

The endocrine system produces hormones and controls your growth and mood.

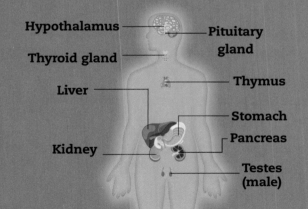

- Hypothalamus
- Thyroid gland
- Liver
- Kidney
- Pituitary gland
- Thymus
- Stomach
- Pancreas
- Testes (male)

- Ovaries (female)

Lymphatic system

The lymphatic system fights off germs and helps keep your body healthy.

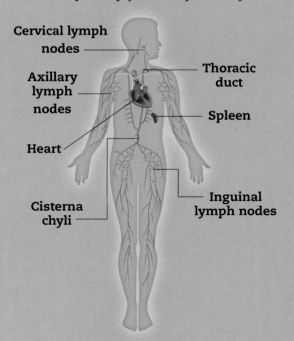

- Cervical lymph nodes
- Axillary lymph nodes
- Heart
- Cisterna chyli
- Thoracic duct
- Spleen
- Inguinal lymph nodes

GLOSSARY

abdomen The area of your body just above and below your belly button. It contains your stomach, intestines, and several other major organs.

appendix A pouch attached to the end of the large intestine.

capillaries Small blood vessels.

cardiac muscles Muscles in the heart.

cartilage Bendy tissue that acts as a shock absorber where the bones meet the joints.

coccyx The tailbone – the lowest part of your backbone.

dentin The layer beneath the enamel in your teeth, which contains nerves and blood.

dermis The layer of skin beneath the epidermis.

diaphragm The muscle beneath the lungs that controls breathing.

enamel The hard outer layer that protects your teeth.

epidermis The outer later of the skin.

femur The long bone in your upper leg.

follicle A tube-shaped cavity that contains the root of a hair.

gene A combination of chemicals that carries information about how an organism will appear and behave.

incisors The sharp teeth at the front of the mouth used to cut food into small pieces.

involuntary muscles The muscles that work without any conscious control, for example the muscles that keep your heart beating.

keratin A tough protein found in hair and nails.

ligaments A band of strong tissue that connects the ends of bones or holds an organ in place.

marrow The soft tissue inside sections of large bone where new blood cells are produced.

melanin The pigment that gives human skin, hair and eyes their color.

molars The broad teeth at the back of the mouth that grind food.

organ A collection of cells that work together to perform a specific function.

pore A structure in the skin that produces sweat.

premolars The broad teeth between the front and back of the mouth that grind food.

protein One of the most important of all molecules in the body, protein is needed to strengthen and replace tissue in the body.

pupil (in the eye) The hole in the center of the iris that allows light to enter the eye. It constantly expands and contracts depending on the amount of light available.

sesamoid bone A bone that is embedded in a tendon.

sinuses The hollow areas in your face behind your nose and cheeks.

skeletal muscles Muscles that are attached to your bones.

skeleton The framework of bones that gives the body its shape and structure.

smooth muscles Muscles found in hollow organs such as blood vessels, the intestines, and the bladder.

spine The backbone.

tendon A tough tissue that connects a muscle to a bone.

tonsils Two small glands on either side of the throat.

trachea (windpipe) The tube that connects the pharynx to the lungs.

voluntary muscles The muscles that are directed by the brain.

wisdom teeth An extra set of molars that come out usually around 20 years of age.

FURTHER READING

Body Works by Anna Claybourne (QED Publishing, 2014)

Everything You Need to Know about the Human Body by Patricia MacNair (Kingfisher, 2011)

Horrible Science: Body Owner's Handbook by Nick Arnold (Scholastic Press, 2014)

How Your Body Works: Moving your Body by Philip Morgan (Franklin Watts, 2011)

Mind Webs: Human Body by Anna Claybourne (Wayland, 2014)

Project Science: Human Body by Sally Hewitt (Franklin Watts, 2012)

INDEX